DARRELL JACKSON

A Practical Checklist for Christian Singles

Contributor/Editor: Joseph Chinn
Editor: Tony Byrne
Book Cover: Anointing Productions
Interior Formatting: Anointing Productions & Darrell Jackson

Ergon Publishing
PO Box 709
Fresno, Texas 77545
www.raiseperformancegroup.com

ISBN: 979-8-218-20948-3

1st Edition / 2024

Table of Contents

Acknowledgments

"To all who are near and dear to me, who have made me the person that you see. To all who have taken the time to pray for me, and to push me to become the man God designed me to be. To all who have gone before me, whose lives have inspired me to reach beyond what others have believed, I love you and thank you all for giving me the encouragement and freedom to dream!"

This workbook is dedicated to all my family and friends who have played a significant part in my life and ministry. While there are many whose names may not appear in these acknowledgements due to the length it would add to this document, their contributions in my life are very important to me, to which I say to them all again… Thank you for doing your part to make me better!

However, I would like to acknowledge a few people who have in their own way inspired and encouraged me in life, and more specifically to complete this manual:

To my wife Marsha, who has extended her love, grace, and patience to me. She knows first-hand and personally understands the implications of the material presented in this manual. Because now, after all that she knows about me after 30 years of marriage, she would agree that having the information in this manual, would have spared her the pain of marrying me…laugh people…it's a joke.

To Dr. Nicolas Ellen and Dr. Mark Haywood, who encouraged me to begin chronicling and publishing the information that I have written for over 25 years.

To my brother Joseph Chinn, who has served as a copy editor and contributor to this manual.

To my accountability partners Kenneth Basile and Minister Daryl Woods (before he went home to be with the Lord), who have always prayed for and pushed me to use "all" of my gifts in ministry.

To Elder Royce Robinson and Joanna Berry, who God used to "provoke me to good works!"

To Pastor Blake Wilson and Elder Harold Washington, who have pointed me to Jesus over the years.

THANK YOU ALL!

- Pastor Darrell Jackson -

BE SURE TO READ THE NEXT 9 PAGES BEFORE YOU PROCEED!

Introduction

How Did We Get Here?

In the Spring of 2010, I was approached by one of the single women in a church I pastored, whom we will call Mary. After church, Mary made her way to me and said, "Pastor, the sermon was just for me, and I need your help. I am currently dating a man whom I have known for a very short time. I want to get married someday, and I am tired of meeting men, dating them, and then after a few months, we go our separate ways. Besides, I am approaching forty, and I am not getting any younger! So, this time, before things get too serious, I want to be sure that he is the right man for me. What should I do?"

So, after pausing for a moment, I replied, "Sister, thanks for sharing this information with me, and for desiring to respect yourself, and honor God. This is a great question, and I am willing to do what I can to help." I then began sharing some practical information about relationships with her. I asked questions about the man she was dating, and I directed her to various biblical passages that she could reference. But after a moment, I noticed that she seemed a bit overwhelmed with all the information that I shared.

After hearing her sigh, almost immediately, I heard the Holy Spirit speak to me, and so I told Mary, "You know what, I have an idea. How would you like to have a tool that you could reference at your leisure, that could help you to think practically and critically about this relationship and others?" To which Mary replied, "Oh, yes… I think this would be a great idea. I want to get married soon, and I would like to have as much information as possible on the front end before I say, 'I Do!'" We chuckled, then I told Mary that I would have something for her in a few days.

A few days after our initial conversation, I sent a portion of the following material that is contained in this manual to Mary. To my amazement, about 4 hours after I sent it to her, Mary told me that she had already peered through the content, made some preliminary decisions about her relationship based on what she read, and that she had sent the information to one of her friends. Now, I was beyond excited and grateful that I had followed the Holy Spirit's lead. I then expressed my gratitude to Mary, and we set up a time to talk further.

About 2 weeks later, the man that Mary was dating came to church with her. I guess the pressure he was under while going through this material with Mary encouraged him to make his courtesy visit to church. During our follow up meeting that week, Mary told me that she was actively engaged in using the material to determine if she would continue dating this man. Then, after about 2 months,

Mary and I talked again, and to my surprise, Mary had made up her mind that she was going to end the relationship. Thus, shortly thereafter, Mary ended the relationship and began being discipled by a seasoned Christian woman to help her grow spiritually, emotionally, and mentally. Additionally, because of this encounter with Mary, her story became the impetus for me to write this workbook.

Ready, Set, Go

The ending to Mary's story is not the norm for many people who are involved in what I call "urgent relationships." I use the term "urgent relationships" because in my experience, these types of relationships are usually formed quickly without any thought of the stakes involved. These types of relationships are also often formed out of a desperate need to feel loved, to fill a void, or simply to fit in with what seems to be normal and acceptable communal behavior.

Because she was getting older, Mary initially believed that she needed to rush past the "Attraction Stage" of seeing and surveying the person of interest, to the "Attachment Stage" of sexual intimacy, which should only occur in the context of a marital relationship. And sadly, most of the time, the story ending for those who skip the foundational stages usually ends with emotional damage because of unfulfilled and unmet expectations after entering an abusive or unbiblical relationship. Therefore, whether you are considering marriage, or simply looking to date, I believe that there is value and wisdom in taking the time to talk through as many personal issues, aspirations, and expectations as possible with the person that you are looking to share time with.... Especially if marriage is in view!

In an article called "Why Pre-Engagement Counseling is a Good Idea for Young Couples," published in 2016 by a dating site called *Christian Mingle*, Andrew Hess wrote about the important impact that pre-marital counseling has in a relationship. For those contemplating marriage, Hess argued that couples should consider taking pre-marital counseling before getting engaged to be married. Hess wrote:

> I believe that many couples considering marriage counseling during engagement might be too late. Some of the issues that come up in premarital counseling would be better discussed and considered before engagement. I wonder if many couples should seek wise counsel before they make the decision to get engaged...
>
> Part of the reason I prefer seeking help before the proposal is that engagement is a time of increased pressures. Planning a wedding and preparing to transition from single life to married life can be stressful on its own. It's not the time to figure out if marriage is really the right move. Too many couples see engagement as a time where you can still decide not to marry.
>
> One of the purposes of good counseling is to help the couple identify and respond to any reasons they might not want to move forward. But many couples get so far into the wedding planning

> that they feel pressure to move forward merely because of all the time and money they've already invested. Pre-engagement counseling means that, instead of facing these questions and the pressure of planning a wedding, you're able to tackle one thing at a time…
>
> I think engagement is better if a 100% commitment to each other is firmly in place. Engagement is about preparing for marriage, not deciding if you want to marry. An engaged couple should have gone through pre-engagement counseling and worked through all the reasons they might want to the rethink the match. Only then should they decide together to move forward. If a couple is going to decide not to get married, the sooner they make that decision, the better.[1]

Although Hess's counseling philosophy may seem ridiculous to some, I believe that at the heart of his argument is a lot of wisdom. For over 30 years, I have offered this model to many couples because I believe that it is healthy for those involved in the relationship, and for those who support the newly formed relationship. I simply believe that "getting the facts" about your potential mate's beliefs and behavior before you begin "spending the stacks" on them will help save a lot of time, money, energy, and embarrassment in the long run. Unfortunately, I have counseled many Christian and non-Christian couples alike who were either in a dating, pre-marital, or post-marital context whose relationships ended in an ugly manner. But I believe that we can change the paradigm and break the cycle!

Are you a single Christian with a desire to date or to be married? Have you been in a long or short-term relationship that seems to be going nowhere fast? Do you feel like the person you are dating is not the person you initially met? As a Christian single, how are you assessing the spiritual, social, mental, or emotional health of the person you are considering dating or even marrying? Better yet, are you spiritually and emotionally ready to date or to get married? Well, it is time to put in the real work, and begin discovering the answers to these questions… "Before You Go Too Far!"

The facts are that not every person will be married. And while it is not wrong to be married or even to desire being married, the same holds true as it relates to being single. Because of varying reasons, there are some people who desire or choose to remain single. In Matthew 19:9–12, Jesus told His disciples that there were some who would be celibate or single. And in 1 Corinthians 7:6–7, 32–34, the Apostle Paul does not say that it is wrong to be married, but he does share with those who are single the benefits of being single.

If you choose to be single, then that is great, or if you choose to marry, then that is also commendable. However, if you are a Christian single, one of the goals of this workbook is to give you a practical tool to help "demystify" the way forward as it relates to engaging in or strengthening your future relationships.

1 Andrew Hess, "Why Pre-Engagement Counseling Is A Smart Idea For Young Couples," *Believe by Christian Mingle*, August 29, 2016, https://www.christianmingle.com/en/believe/love/relationships/pre-engagement-counseling.

Because of the practical information that it possesses, this workbook is a tool that many colleagues of mine and I wished we had access to before we started dating or considered being married. The principles that are presented and the personal reflection section in each Checkpoint helps you to think through and to ask the critical questions that should be talked through first, before you consider dating or even marriage.

So, whichever place you find yourself in on the journey, our encouragement to you through the material in this manual is to:

- Slow down,
- Settle your emotions,
- Submit yourself to God, and
- Start the process of putting in the work required.

Please remember that there are no shortcuts when it comes to building long-lasting, sustainable, life-giving, and God-honoring relationships. The "work phase" is an area that must not be neglected. So, for the sake of your future, and God's glory, please take the time to work through the material in this manual seriously, patiently, and prayerfully. Ask, and do your best to answer the deep questions, which will help you better understand both yourself and the person you are dating, desiring to date, or marry.

Lastly, please beware that after you work through the material in this manual, that your perspective on and interest in the relationship might change, which is perfectly fine. Allow the Holy Spirit the freedom to speak to your heart, and the heart of the person you are entering into a relationship with "Before You Go Too Far!"

About This Manual

Before you say "I Do" to a future relationship, wisdom says that you should take time to know the real you, and to do your due diligence with respect to the person you are dating, desiring to date, or marry in the future. Because many people make *emotional* investments in a relationship without ever considering *practical* data about themselves or about the person of interest, the information in this manual was written as a proactive way to combat the collateral damage that can occur because of this type of behavior.

Before We Go Too Far: A Practical Checklist for Christian Singles **is designed to help Christian Singles:**

- Assess their spiritual, social, mental, or emotional health, and that of the person they are dating, considering dating, or even marrying through intentional conversations,
- Establish clear godly boundaries that can in essence guard against sinful lust patterns and superficial attractions,
- Engage in intentional conversations with spiritual mentors who will be devoted to journey with and pray for them,
- Glorify God through their thoughts, words, and deeds.

Because no one will ever know everything about themselves, or about another person before they date or marry them, the information presented in this manual is not designed to be exhaustive, or to give you all the answers. It is, however, designed help you make a "faith decision" about the future that is informed by prayer and wise counsel (i.e., spiritual mentors, the Bible, etc.). This resource is a way for you to gather as many facts as possible about your life and the person you are dating, desiring to date, or marry.

How to Use This Manual

The information in this manual is designed to serve as a tool to assist you with making both "observational evaluations" and "conversational realizations" that will surface concerning you and your future partner. It is designed to be a sort of "personal coach" or "cheat sheet" that helps you to "fact find" and grow over time.

During the time that you will spend prayerfully "observing" and "talking" through the critical areas that are presented in this manual, our prayer is that the information contained in this manual will assist you in learning more about who you both are mentally, emotionally, habitually, and spiritually. The goal is "transformation" in each area of your life, and not just the acquisition of more "information."

So please use the information presented as:

- A guide to deeper discussions concerning you, and the person you are dating, desiring to date or marry,
- A way to discover obvious attitudes and actions that you, and the person you are dating, desiring to date, or marry may possess,
- A discipling tool for you, and for the person you are dating, desiring to date, or marry (If there is a mentor involved, then they can also use this information to help navigate the journey).

The chapters in this manual are called **Checkpoints**. Other than the Helpful Resources section at the end of this workbook, the **Checkpoint sections** contain one or more of the following sections:

- **Point to Ponder:** Helps shape your mind for the material in each section.
- **Tune-Ups:** Sub-sections in the chapters
    - **Putting in the Work:** Helps engage your head, heart, and hands through a series of practical exercises.
    - **Putting Things into Perspective:** Helps drive home the message of the work engaged in through a series of questions.
    - **Prayer Time:** Helps connect you to the Lord in Whom you will find the wisdom and strength needed to apply the lessons learned.

ICON LEGEND

TUNE-UPS: This icon denotes the major sections in a chapter.

This icon denotes the sub sections under each major section in a chapter.
NOTE: You will also see smaller sections under each sub section.

QUESTIONS TO CONSIDER: This icon denotes the questions section in a chapter.
NOTE: All Scripture references used in this manual will be from the New King James Version (NKJV) or New American Standard 1995 Version (NASB) of the Bible.

How to Approach Each Section

To allow for open, honest, and transparent engagement with the material in each section, please allow the following timelines to act as a guide as you respond thoughtfully and intentionally to the material. The approximate times are suggested to allow you space to learn more about yourself, and time to observe your potential mate with intentionality in several contexts naturally without coercion. Our hope is that you will engage in genuine conversation in the natural rhythm of your relationship.

The Suggested Time Commitment

We believe 17–21 weeks is a reasonable amount of time to invest focused energy into a relationship that you are serious about. Especially for those considering marriage, which God sees as a life-long covenant (Gen. 2:24; Matt. 19:4–6; 1 Cor. 7:9–11). From our own research, and from the studies we have obtained from various relational experts, the data shows that those couples who choose to intentionally invest in their relationship from the beginning are usually better equipped to communicate and to face the challenges that arise.

Of course, you can complete the work in this manual at the pace that you deem appropriate. However, our recommended range of 17–21 weeks has been suggested to help you fully engage in the information presented through prayer, meaningful conversations, and personal reflection.

Here is our recommended overview:

Checkpoint #1—Who Am I?	Approximately 1 week
Checkpoint #2—How Do You See Them Now? Pre-Survey Questions	Approximately 1–2 weeks
Checkpoint #3—General Profile Questions	Approximately 7 total weeks (1 week per category)
Checkpoint #4—Male & Female Specific Questions	Approximately 2 weeks (1 per set of questions)
Checkpoint #5—Extras: Let's Talk About It	Approximately 4–6 weeks
Checkpoint #6—How Do You See Them Now? Post-Survey Questions	Approximately 2 weeks
Checkpoint #7—What Have You Discovered?	Approximately 1–2 weeks
Helpful Tools	As needed
** Depending on what stage you are in relationally (i.e., dating, widowed, contemplating remarriage, etc.), you might find it helpful to spend concentrated time in one or on a combination of checkpoints, versus initially going through the entire manual. Scan the material and figure out what works for you in your context, and then work accordingly.	

Who am I?

Checkpoint #1

Who Am I?

Point to Ponder

I have heard stories of people who have dreamed of being married since they were children, only to grow up, and begin a dating relationship that did not last 6–12 months. Couples I have spoken to who have experienced this type of short-lived relationship, oftentimes say that: (1) they met the real person they were dating after some time and couldn't handle what they saw, (2) they were trying to make the other person become something they wanted but failed, or (3) through a series of events the individual discovered that they were not ready to commit because their life was broken and needed to be repaired; they did not know who they were!

Many people are good at seeing how much someone else needs to change but can't at all see the holes in their own life. However, before we begin pointing fingers at others, we should first look at ourselves in the mirror to discover and repair the areas that are damaged by our past and present so that we can become whole.

PUTTING IN THE WORK

"O Lord, You have searched me and known me. You know my sitting down and my rising up. You understand my thought afar off. You comprehend my path and my lying down, and are acquainted with all my ways."

Psalm 139:1–3 NKJV

We encourage you to take some time to engage in personal introspection and discovery before you begin meeting with the person you are dating, desiring to date, or marry to begin discussing the future of your relationship and your assessments of them (Ps. 139:23–24; Matt. 7:1–5).

This time could be spent in some alone time, with a trusted friend or mentor, or between a combination of the two with a specific focus on discovering:

- Your own spiritual, mental, and emotional health needs, and
- Any attitudes and actions that could threaten intimacy and communication.

It is often very difficult for people to see the harmful areas that are present in their hearts and minds due to sin, past trauma, or interpersonal conflicts. Nor do they know their unique qualities and God-given purpose, simply because the individual has never spent the time needed to know who they are and how they are wired.

Therefore, this section is designed to assist you in "seeing you" and your unique skills and abilities to give you a snapshot of the real person staring back at you in the mirror. After working through the information in this section, you should have a better answer to the question, "Who Am I?"

In this section, we will explore three areas:

1. **The Real YOU Personally: Who Do I Say I Am?** How **YOU** see you: **Uniquely You** is an assessment tool that is designed to assist in knowing both your natural abilities and spiritual gifts.
2. **The Real YOU Communally: Who Do They Say I Am?** How **YOU & OTHERS** see you: The **Johari Window** is a communication tool designed to assist in increasing your self-awareness, self-perception, and mutual understanding with others.
3. **The Real YOU Biblically: Who Does God Say I Am?** How **GOD** sees you: The **Bible** is God's Word in which we will use selected passages in the **Biblical Insights** section in order to give God's truth about you and your purpose.

1.1 – The Real YOU Personally: Who Do I Say I Am?

We all have a personal perspective about our abilities that may not be accurate. The Uniquely You Profiler is a cutting-edge online tool that details your personalized spiritual gifts and DISC Personality Temperaments, to help you gain a clearer understanding of your unique personality, gifts, and abilities.

In this section you will complete a **Uniquely You assessment called *Combining 16 Spiritual Gifts and 4 DISC Personality Types Online Profile*.** In it, you will be asked a series of quick questions. After you complete the assessments, you will receive your results immediately online through a personalized report that reveals your top 3 primary Spiritual Gifts, as well as your primary DISC Personality Temperament. **There is a one-time cost associated with taking this assessment. Both you and the person you are entering into a relationship with should complete separate assessments.**

- **Important Note:** *In order to receive accurate results, please answer each question honestly. Please do not answer the questions from a standpoint of how you would "prefer or aspire to be." Instead, accurately answer each question based on how you currently feel about a situation.* The goal is to have accurate results.
- **Please navigate to the website below to purchase and complete the assessment:**

  www.raiseperformancegroup.com

  - Select the **Resource** button at the top of the website. Under the drop down select Uniquely You
  - Scroll down to the **Purchase the Assessment Here** button and click the button
  - On the next page, select the **Add to Cart** button
  - Next, select the appropriate quantity of assessments you need, then click the **Checkout** button
  - On the next page, click the **Register Now** button and follow the prompts to create your free account with Uniquely You
  - Complete the checkout process
  - Complete the assessment
- Once you complete the online assessment, please answer the questions below.

Please contact us at Raise Performance Group if you need assistance with purchasing the assessment. Our contact information can be found at the end of this manual.

Questions to Consider (DISC Section)

Although God has wired each of us uniquely, He still requires us to relate to one another with respect and compassion according to the Fruit of the Spirit (Gal. 5:22–26). To help you gain a clearer understanding of your personality, use your assessment results to answer the following questions.

1. What are your two Behavior Blends? (Example: IC, DI, etc.)
   -
   -

2. What are the top three things that you learned about your Behavior Blends?
   - How do you respond under pressure?
   - Are you more "task" or "people" oriented?
   - How do you think internally?

3. What do these behaviors tell you about how you communicate and relate to others?

4. In view of your future relationship, and based on your results, is there a behavior pattern that you notice about yourself that needs to change? If so, define the behavior pattern and explain how you will change it.

Questions to Consider (SPIRITUAL GIFTS Section)

God has given all believers spiritual gifts in order to glorify Him and edify other believers (Rom. 1:11–12; 1 Cor. 12:7-11; Eph. 4:11–16), but we must know what our gifts are and use them tirelessly and with joy. To help you maximize your spiritual gift(s), use your assessment results to answer the following questions.

1. What are your top three spiritual gifts?
   -
   -
   -

2. How are you currently using your spiritual gift(s) in service for God and others?

3. Which gift(s) do you use the most, or are you the most comfortable using?

4. How could you begin increasing the use of your spiritual gift(s) in service for God and others?

5. Which gift(s) do you use the least, or are you the least comfortable using? How will you change that?

6. How have you seen God use your spiritual gift(s) to edify and encourage other believers?

7. Did this assessment reveal anything about your spiritual gift(s) that was surprising? If so, describe your findings.

1.2 – The Real YOU Communally: Who Do They Say I Am?

One of the ways to ensure that we are growing in our relationship with others, and in our ability to know how others view our attitudes and actions, is to be open to receiving honest feedback. The Johari Window is a model that assists groups and individuals in understanding the conscious and unconscious biases they possess, with the goal of increasing their self-awareness and understanding of themselves and others.

The information in this section has been adapted from the Johari Window model. In the adapted version, we will use <u>three</u> of the <u>four</u>-quadrants (***Open Area, Blind Area, Hidden Area***, ***Unknown Area***) as a guide to help you grow in your self-awareness and relationship with others, by inviting you to receive feedback from others about your blind spots. In this section we will focus primarily on the first three (3) quadrants.

Instructions: Complete this exercise with the person you are dating, desiring to date, or marry (Prov. 27:5–6).

- Please read the descriptions of each quadrant.
- In the chart provided called "**The Mirror**,"[2] allow the person completing this exercise with you to list at least 2 behaviors that they notice about you in the section (*Name It, Explain It, Steps to Improve It or Remove It*).
- Afterwards, answer the questions that follow.

The goal of this exercise is to help you become naked and unashamed (Gen. 2:23–25), more aware of your skills, limitations, attitudes, and actions, and to give you feedback on how to address these areas. Because we are sinful (Jer. 17:9–10; Rom. 3:23; James 4:1–10), our usual tendency is to know what others need to do to get better, while failing to see areas in which we need improvement.

(Further study on the Johari Window can be conducted at your leisure. Some of the four-quadrants explanation information below has been adapted from Mindtools.com)

Overview of the Johari Window's Four-Quadrants

1. **Open Area**—represents things that you and others know about you.
2. **Blind Area**—represents things that you don't know about you, but that others do know about you.
3. **Hidden Area**—represents things that you know about yourself, but that you keep hidden from other people.
4. **Unknown Area**—represents things that are unknown to you and others but are revealed to you as you experience life.

Note: The four-quadrants can change size over time, and because they are interdependent, changing the size of one quadrant will also change the size of the others. For example, telling your team (*or for our purposes your future partner*) about an aspect of your life that you would always keep hidden would decrease your Hidden Area and increase your Open Area.[3]

2 The Mirror Chart: Created by Darrell Jackson for Raise Performance Group.

3 Mind Tools Content Team, "The Johari Window: Building Self-Awareness and Trust," *MindTools*, accessed January 2, 2024, https://www.mindtools.com/au7v71d/the-johari-window.

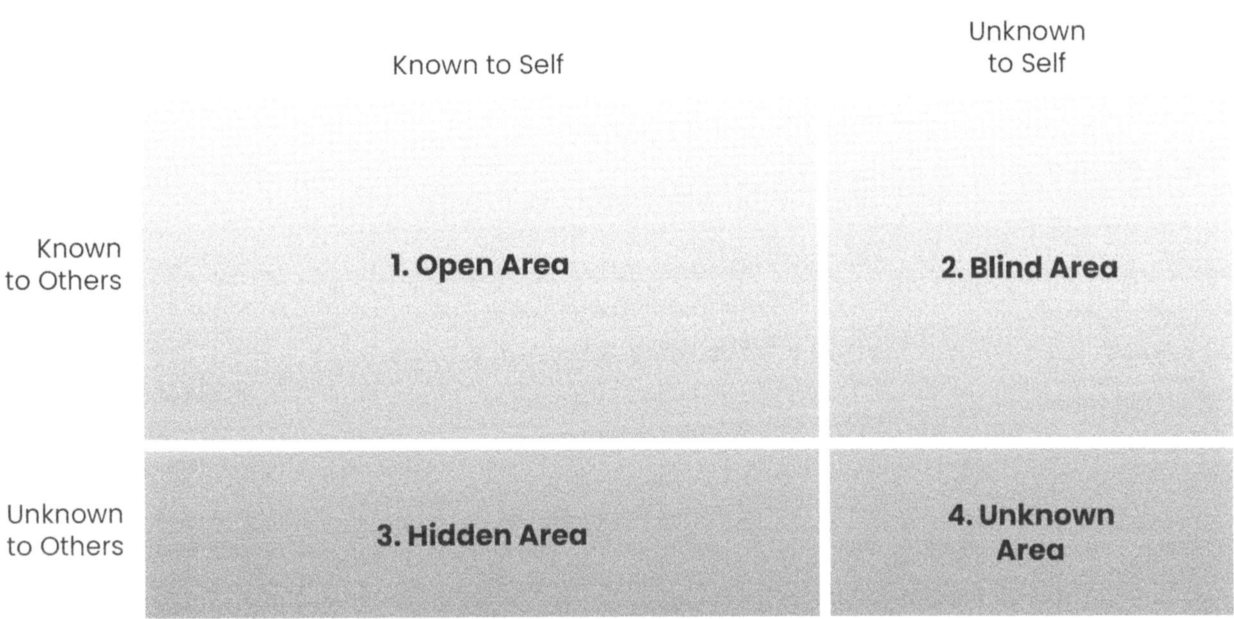

An Ideal Johari Window 4-quadrants adapted from Mindtools.com.

The Mirror

Now let's take some time to explore the Four-Quadrants in more detail to discover how YOU and OTHERS see you. Each quadrant will have specific instructions and a specific focus.

Quadrant #1 – The Open Area

- **Focus Area of This Quadrant:** YOU & OTHERS
- **Instructions:** Read the description of this quadrant, then use the Mirror chart below to better understand how YOU & OTHERS see you. List at least two (2) positive or negative behaviors that you or the person completing this section with you notice about YOU. An example has been provided to help complete this section. Use additional paper if needed.
- **Description of the Open Area**—represents things that you and others know about you.
  - **Example:** Feelings, Behaviors, Knowledge, Skills, Attitudes, etc.
  - **Aim:** Your aim is to increase the size of your Open Area through appropriate self-disclosure, shared discovery, and feedback. The more people know about themselves and others, the better their relationships can be.

Known to Self

Known to Others

1. Open Area

- **Insights:** Because they have not shared much information about themselves, Small Open Areas can be a sign that someone is young, new to the relationship, not very self-aware, an introvert, uncommunicative, or difficult to work with.

THE MIRROR ©

Person Recognizing Your Behavior	Name It	Explain It	Steps to Improve It and/or Remove It
The Person I'm Dating	1. Good Communicator	• I have noticed that you are a very good communicator under normal circumstances. You have an amazing ability to simplify complex subjects for your audience.	• Continue to be mindful of your audience and the need to make complex topics simple to understand.
• The Person I'm Dating • Me	2. People Pleaser	• I have noticed that you tend to go along to get along by agreeing with the details of conversations in which you have a difference of opinion. • I have noticed that I tend to remain silent during high emotional conversations.	• Speak up and state your opinion. • Don't look for validation, but seek to let your voice be heard.

Now, spend some time on the next page to complete The Mirror exercise. To record your answers, please use the Notes section at the end of this chapter, or additional paper if necessary.

THE MIRROR ©			
Person Recognizing Your Behavior	Name It	Explain It	Steps to Improve It and/or Remove It
	1.	•	•
	2.	•	•
	3.	•	•

Questions to Consider (JOHARI WINDOW – Open Area Section)

1. Explain what you have learned about yourself that could positively/negatively impact your relationship(s).

2. Explain what you believe are the long-term relational effects of what you have learned about yourself.

3. Explain what opportunities you have missed or gained based on the information you have discovered.

4. Explain what measures you have/are putting in place to continue growing in this area.

Open Area Section Wrap-Up & Additional Information

Use this section to list any other behaviors you have learned about yourself.

___

___

___

___

___

Quadrant #2 – The Blind Area

- **Focus Area of This Quadrant:** OTHERS
- **Instructions:** Read the description of this quadrant, then use the Mirror chart below to better understand specifically how OTHERS see you. Ask the person completing this section with you to list at least two (2) positive or negative behaviors that they notice about YOU. An example has been provided to help complete this section. Use additional paper if needed.

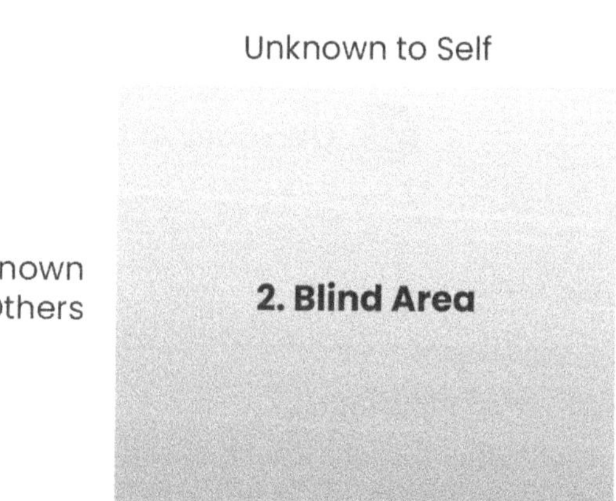

- **Description of the Blind Area**—represents things that you don't know about you, but that others do know about you.
    - **Example:** Rude, Poor Listener, Nervous Habits, an Encourager, etc.
    - **Aim:** Because no one functions best in the dark, your aim is to reduce your Blind Area by welcoming feedback from others.

- **Insights:** Small Blind Areas indicate that you are aware of how your behavior affects other people, whereas a large Blind Area suggests that you may be naïve or even in denial about it. A large Blind Area could also mean that your colleagues are keeping what they know about you to themselves.

THE MIRROR ©			
Person Recognizing Your Behavior	Name It	Explain It	Steps to Improve It and/or Remove It
My Fiancé	1. Insensitive	• I have noticed that you are not aware of the negative effects that you have on your kids. Your kids are afraid to speak up because of your domineering presence.	• Ask for honest feedback from me after a family meeting about your approach and/or tone.
My Brother	2. Blaming Others	• I have noticed that in several conversations, you tend to blame everyone for the events that occur in your life.	• Take responsibility for your own actions. • Talk to a counselor to help you deal with issues in your past.

EXAMPLE

Now, spend some time on the next page to complete The Mirror exercise. To record your answers, please use the Notes section at the end of this chapter, or additional paper if necessary.

THE MIRROR ©			
Person Recognizing Your Behavior	Name It	Explain It	Steps to Improve It and/or Remove It
	1.	•	•
	2.	•	•
	3.	•	•

Questions to Consider (JOHARI WINDOW/Blind Area Section)

1. Explain what you have learned about yourself that could positively/negatively impact your relationship(s).

2. Explain what you believe are the long-term relational effects of what you have learned about yourself.

3. Explain what opportunities you have missed or gained based on the information you have discovered.

4. Explain what measures you have/are putting in place to continue growing in this area.

Blind Area Section Wrap-Up & Additional Information

Use this section to list any other things you have learned about yourself.

____

____

____

____

____

Quadrant #3 – The Hidden Area

- **Focus Area of This Quadrant:** YOU
- **Instructions:** Read the description of this quadrant, then use the Mirror chart below to better understand specifically how <u>YOU</u> see yourself. As you are comfortable with disclosing, list at least two (2) positive or negative behaviors that no one knows about YOU. An example has been provided to help you complete this section. Use additional paper if needed.

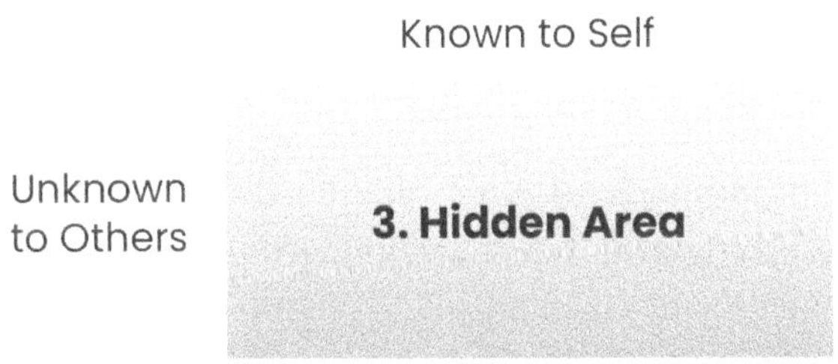

	Known to Self
Unknown to Others	**3. Hidden Area**

- **Description of the Hidden Area**—represents things that you know about yourself, but that you keep hidden from other people.

  - **Example:** Embarrassing Moments, Personal or Family Medical History, Financial Issues, Your Human Side, etc.
  - **Aim:** Although you do not need to share all of your private thoughts and feelings with people you work with, or when in a relationship, your aim should be to share openly with your partner so as to increase trust. Proper self-disclosure can lead to deeper levels of trust, understanding, and collaboration.

- **Insights:** Large Hidden Areas can decrease the communication and trust level that you have with others over time. Therefore, the goal is to communicate and decrease your Hidden Area by not keeping secrets or being driven by anxious thoughts (i.e., what they will see about you, or how they will view you, etc.).

THE MIRROR ©			
Person Recognizing Your Behavior	Name It	Explain It	Steps to Improve It and/or Remove It
Me	1. Insecurity	• I fear looking weak in front of my boss and co-workers, so instead of asking for help, I tend to tackle projects alone, which causes me to have a lot of mistakes, and even fail to meet deadlines.	• Focus more attention on the things that I do well, and gradually work to improve areas I am weak in. • Ask for help
Me	2. Raped	• I was raped by my uncle when I was 10 years old, and so I don't want to have sex, or tell anyone about it.	• Get professional counseling • Stop blaming myself

Now, spend some time on the next page to complete The Mirror exercise. To record your answers, please use the Notes section at the end of this chapter, or additional paper if necessary.

THE MIRROR ©			
Person Recognizing Your Behavior	Name It	Explain It	Steps to Improve It and/or Remove It
	1.	•	•
	2.	•	•
	3.	•	•

Questions to Consider (JOHARI WINDOW/Hidden Area Section)

1. Explain what you have learned about yourself that could positively/negatively impact your relationship(s).

2. Explain what you believe are the long-term relational effects of what you have learned about yourself.

3. Explain what opportunities you have missed or gained based on the information you have discovered.

4. Explain what measures you have/are putting in place to continue growing in this area.

Hidden Area Section Wrap-Up & Additional Information

Use this section to list any other things you have learned about yourself.

____

____

____

____

____

Quadrant #4 – The Unknown Area

- **Focus Area of This Quadrant:** YOU
- **Instructions:** Read the description of this quadrant, then use the Mirror chart below to better understand new discoveries that <u>YOU</u> are making about yourself as you experience life. List at least two (2) positive or negative behaviors that you are discovering about YOU. An example has been provided to help complete this section. Use additional paper if needed.

	Unknown to Self
Unknown to Others	**4. Unknown Area**

- **Description of the Unknown Area**—represents things that are unknown to you and others but are revealed to you as you experience life.
  - **Example:** Thoughts, Feelings, Ambitions, Untapped Abilities, Preferences, etc.
  - **Aim:** Although you do not need to share all of your private information, it is good to let others know when you have discovered something new about yourself. Information is waiting to be shared. Not only will your Open Area become larger, but celebratory moments and points of clarity will increase.

- **Insights**: A large Unknown Area may just be a sign of youth or inexperience, but it can also mean that you need to work hard on discovering and releasing new information about yourself.

THE MIRROR ©			
Person Recognizing Your Behavior	Name It	Explain It	Steps to Improve It and/or Remove It
Me	1. Camping/Fishing	• I went camping with my friend and realized that I enjoyed the outdoors, and I am a pretty good fisherman.	• Be more open to taking outdoor trips and to learn something new.
Me	2. Claustrophobic	• I rode a rollercoaster at the Amusement Park last week with my nephew and discovered that I am afraid of tight spaces.	• I will reflect on my childhood to discover any reason(s) I am this way, and for now, I won't ride rollercoasters.

EXAMPLE

Now, spend some time on the next page to complete The Mirror exercise. To record your answers, please use the Notes section at the end of this chapter, or additional paper if necessary.

THE MIRROR ©			
Person Recognizing Your Behavior	Name It	Explain It	Steps to Improve It and/or Remove It
	1.	•	•
	2.	•	•
	3.	•	•

Questions to Consider (JOHARI WINDOW/Unknown Area Section)

1. Explain what you have learned about yourself that could positively/negatively impact your relationship(s).

2. Explain what you believe are the long-term relational effects of what you have learned about yourself.

3. Explain what opportunities you have missed or gained based on the information you have discovered.

4. Explain what measures you have/are putting in place to continue growing in this area.

Unknown Area Section Wrap-Up & Additional Information

Use this section to list any other things you have learned about yourself.

____
____
____
____
____

 1.3 – The Real YOU Biblically: Who Does God Say I Am?

When we are saved by faith through the Gospel of Jesus, we are transferred by the power of the Holy Spirit from spiritual death to spiritual life (1 Cor. 15:1–4; 2 Cor. 5:17; Eph. 2). Regardless of how you feel or what others tell you, one of the most powerful tools for the believer is to live each day with a deep awareness and appreciation of their identity from God's perspective. Although we live in a day of a plethora of opinions, the only truth that really matters is what God has to say about us!

However, before we can see others clearly, we must replace our skewed view of ourselves with who God sees when He looks at us (Matt. 7:1–5; Rom. 8:17, 37; 2 Cor. 5:20-21; Eph. 2:6, 19). Read each Bible passage and write a brief summary that describes how God sees you based on that passage and commit your Christian identity to memory with gratitude in your heart to God.

To help you get started, finish this statement next to each verse on the lines below: According to these Bible verses, God says that I am…

Genesis 1:26–28

Psalm 139:14

Matthew 5:14–16

John 1:12

John 15:15–16

Romans 8:28–29

Romans 8:37

2 Corinthians 5:17

2 Corinthians 5:20

Colossians 3:12

Galatians 2:20

Ephesians 1:4, 13

Ephesians 2:10

1 Peter 2:9

1 John 3:1–2

Now, considering what God says about you, live your life in light of the truth that God reveals!

PUTTING THINGS INTO PERSPECTIVE

As you answer the questions below, use the biblical passages in the previous section as a point of reference. Use Scripture to shape each of your responses.

1. Explain how you would rate your own spiritual health and maturity (i.e., prayer, Bible reading/study, authentic community, spiritual accountability).

2. Based on the exercise above, explain what steps you will take to engage more meaningfully in your walk with Christ to eradicate any false narratives that you believe about yourself.

3. Explain how your pastor or spiritual mentor would rate your spiritual health and maturity.

4. Explain the ways your behavioral patterns potentially show that you are seeking comfort and significance from this relationship that only God can give.

5. Share your results with the person you are dating, desiring to date or marry, and with your mentor.

PRAYER TIME

Take some time to write down and to pray through at least three (3) areas that were revealed in this section that you need more clarity, direction, or peace on from the Lord. Remember to be specific and honest with the Lord and with yourself. As you are able, share those areas with someone spiritually mature who will help keep you accountable.

Notes for This Section

I HAVE A
CRUSH ON
YOU

Checkpoint #2

How Do You See Them Now? (Pre-Assessment Questions)

Point to Ponder

Many times, when people want to be in a relationship, they will enter the relationship with their eyes "wide shut" and overlook obvious "positive" and "negative" behavior patterns because of their strong desire for companionship.

Because you may not have a lot of previous knowledge about the person you are interested in, this section is designed to help you capture your initial "thoughts" and "feelings" about the person through your personal survey of their observable "Qualitative" and "Questionable" Qualities.

While no one is perfect, and we are all still works in progress, it is imperative that you be prayerful and fair in your assessments. However, please do not overlook the obvious positive and negative things that God may be showing you, because some things about the person's behavior may or may not get better with time!

TUNE-UP 1

PUTTING IN THE WORK

"For through the grace given to me I say to everyone among you not to think more highly of himself than he ought to think, but to think so as to have sound judgment, as God has allotted to each a measure of faith."

Romans 12:3 NASB

1.1 – THE GRID ©

To help you get the most out of this section, please feel free to list other qualities that you see, or feelings that you have that may not be presented in the information provided. Listing as much information as possible in the Grid Chart[4] will be helpful because you will reference it in the last section of this manual.

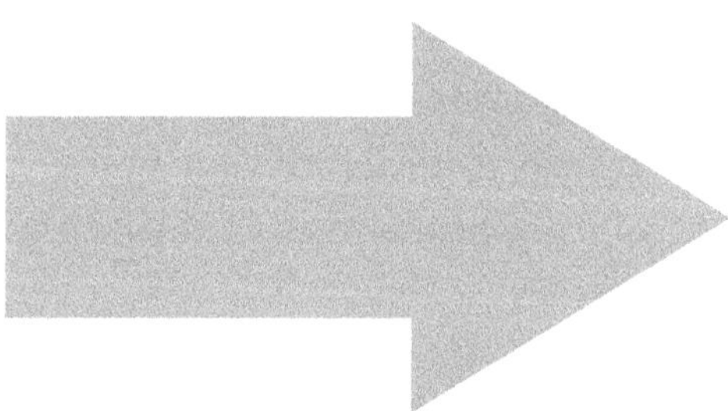

On the Grid Charts, complete Lists 1 & 2 on the next two pages.

4 The Grid Chart: Created by Darrell Jackson for Raise Performance Group.

Instructions: Based on your **"current"** interactions with the individual, place a check by as many areas that describe your <u>initial</u> "thoughts" and "feelings" about the person at this stage of your relationship.

Qualitative Qualities	Questionable Qualities
LIST 1	
___ As an attractive person	___ As an unattractive person
___ As a loyal person	___ As an abuser (drugs, alcohol, people)
___ As a family focused person	___ As an adulterer/fornicator
___ As an active/committed church member	___ As a hit or miss church member
___ As a humble person	___ As a braggart
___ As a charmer	___ As a blunt or direct person
___ As a trustworthy person	___ As a cheater
___ As a conqueror	___ As a complainer
___ As easy-going	___ As a disciplinarian
___ As an informed Christian	___ As a confused Christian
___ As a neat/clean person	___ As a disorderly/dirty person
___ As a mature Christian	___ As a new/immature Christian
___ As a giver	___ As a materialistic person
___ As an encourager/supporter	___ As an envious/jealous person
___ As a good father	___ As a bad father
___ As a good mother	___ As a bad mother
___ As a good family member (sibling, etc.)	___ As a bad family member (sibling, etc.)
___ As a happy person	___ As a miser
___ As a follower	___ As a flirter
___ As a friendly person	___ As an unfriendly person
___ As a forgiver	___ As a resentful/vindictive person
___ As a joyful person	___ As an unhappy person

Qualitative Qualities	Questionable Qualities
LIST 2	
___ As an honest person	___ As a liar
___ As listener	___ As a gossiper
___ As a lover	___ As an enforcer
___ As a leader/influencer	___ As a control freak
___ As good manager of their time	___ As a poor manager of their time
___ As a good manager of their talent	___ As a poor manager of their talent
___ As a good manager of their treasure	___ As a poor manager of their treasure
___ As a missionary	___ As a homebody
___ As an open person	___ As a closed person
___ As a quiet person	___ As a loud person
___ As a responsible person	___ As an irresponsible person
___ As a saver	___ As a spender
___ As one who prioritizes prayer/praise	___ As a nagger
___ As one who is content	___ As a perfectionist
___ As a positive role model	___ As a negative role model
___ As an optimist	___ As a skeptic
___ As an organizer	___ As a lazy person
___ As goal oriented/over-achiever	___ As an under-achiever
___ As a visionary	___ As a fantasy-driven person
___ As a wise person	___ As an unwise person
___ As a confident person	___ As a worrier
___ As one who empowers	___ As one who enables

PUTTING THINGS INTO PERSPECTIVE

Questions to Consider

Instructions: Based on your initial observations of the person, and the categories you have selected above, use this section to answer the questions below about your current perception of the person you are dating, desiring to date, or marry. Please feel free to utilize your coach/mentor as a sounding board for you as you go through this process and use additional paper if needed.

1. Explain your overall feelings about the person after completing the Pre-Assessment (i.e., hopeful, questionable, etc.).

2. Please explain what caused you to choose the categories you selected. Was there a specific incident that occurred?

3. Explain if there were any areas that stood out to you the most about this person.

4. Are there areas you selected that were "your personal goals" for the person to become better in? (i.e., more loving, caring, a better listener, etc.)
   - If so, then why do you want them to achieve this goal? Be specific.

   - If so, then what do you believe their response will be to your aspirations for them?

- If so, then what do you believe your response will be if they never achieve these goals?
- If none, then move on to the next question.

5. Explain if there were any selections you made that caused you to think extra hard about your choices.

6. Explain what excites you the most about the Qualitative Qualities that you selected.

7. Explain what worries you the most about the Questionable Qualities that you selected.

ADDITIONAL QUESTIONS

Use this area to list any other questions that you may have that you need to think through.

PRAYER TIME

Take some time to write down and to pray through at least three (3) areas that were revealed in this section that you need more clarity, direction, or peace from the Lord. Remember to be specific and honest with the Lord and with yourself.

Notes for This Section

Checkpoint #3

General Profile Questions

Point to Ponder

Do you really know the person you have eyes for? Then consider this… For about 5 years, I had the opportunity to work as a Private Investigator (P.I.) for a private firm. And during my time at the company, I learned some valuable investigative skills. One skill that helped me become a successful P.I. at this company is called Skip Tracing. Simply put, Skip Tracing is an action taken to locate people who are deemed "untraceable."

In short, because I was trained to exercise patience while following the clues, ask and answer the right questions, and to leave no stone left unturned while working a case, I was able to find all the details needed about a person, and close most of my cases fast.

When it comes to relationships, although you may not be a trained P.I., I do believe that you should, in a sense, see yourself as a sort of "Relationship P.I.," an investigator who intentionally seeks to ask and answer the right questions of your potential companion to discover important facts about them. Beloved, when it comes to your future, you need to know as many of the facts as possible! Don't miss the "critical clues" needed to assist you in knowing if the person you are interested in is worth the investment of your time and emotional energy!

PUTTING IN THE WORK

"Therefore, be careful how you walk, not as unwise men but as wise, making the most of your time, because the days are evil. So then do not be foolish, but understand what the will of the Lord is."

Ephesians 5:15–17 NASB

Instructions: Below is a <u>summary</u> list of the General Questions Chart[5] that are broken up into seven categories: (1) Conduct (2) Character (3) Conversation (4) Community (5) Commitment (6) Contentment (7) Conversion. This is not an exhaustive list of areas that could be explored, but the information listed is designed to help you take the first steps in asking and answering the right questions by helping you to <u>think critically</u> through some of the "overt" & "covert" (i.e., spiritual, social, mental, emotional) dimensions of your potential mate.

Proverbs 15:1; Matthew 5:13–16; John 14:15; Romans 12:9–21; Galatians 5:22–23; Ephesians 4:25–32; 5:1–4; 1 Corinthians 3:16–17; 6:19–20						
Conduct	Character	Conversation	Community	Commitment	Contentment	Conversion
How do they act?	Are their godly traits evident?	How do they communicate?	How do others see them & engage w/ them?	Who/what are they dedicated to?	What gives them satisfaction?	Have they been changed?
Are they commonly outgoing or reserved?	Is the Fruit of the Spirit consistently displayed in their life?	Is their speech clean and inviting?	Do others see them as a good, bad, lying, loving, etc., person?	Is their seriousness about God and loyalty to Him evident?	Do they know and pursue the secret of contentment?	Does the person know what the gospel is & how to explain it?
Are they always on edge or even tempered?	Are they Christ-like or worldly?	Is the sex topic number one or the Scriptures?	How do their family members view them?	Are they committed to holiness, studying/learning Scripture and to prayer?	Are they satisfied with God's provisions for their life or do they want more?	Does this person actively share their faith?
How do they prefer to solve problems, immediately or by avoidance?	Are they modest, honest, sneaky, or greedy?	Is their speech gentle, encouraging, argumentative, or abusive?	How well do they work with others (jobs, community, sphere of influence)?	Is their job more important than God, their family, or you?	Are they consumed with you and your love?	Is the person saved and growing, saved and carnal, or not saved?
Do they behave ethically & morally?	Are they peacemakers or instigators?	How do they talk to their parents, family, friends, etc.?	Are they seen as a team player or individual player?	What are their goals and aspirations?	Are they secure about themselves or are they needy?	Is their changed life obvious to others?
Will they lie, steal, or cheat to get ahead?	Do they seem more like the wimpy or warrior type?	Is their speech free of flirtatious overtones, threats, degrading remarks, and swearing?	Do they have a network of positive or negative friends?	Are they driven to achieve their dreams at the expense of your family?	Are they happy with themselves and with their responsibilities and roles (i.e., on their jobs, in their homes, and community)?	Is living consistently as a Christian important to them or do they compromise?

<u>PLEASE NOTE:</u> Work through this section with the person that you are dating, desiring to date, or

5 The General Questions Chart: Created by Darrell Jackson for Raise Performance Group.

marry to gather the facts about them firsthand. You will determine the pace and pattern of your progress through this section. It is perfectly okay if other questions may arise as you work through the material. Simply write out those questions and answer them in the space provided. Also, think through areas that are or could be potential obstacles in your relationship.

Please do not ignore the potential trouble areas that these general questions may reveal. Allow the Holy Spirit room to direct you as you think through, answer, and develop solutions to each question under each category. You may also want to work through this material in your pre/post counseling sessions.

Each section will end with a summary section called "WHAT DID I LEARN?" to help you synthesize the information explored in that section.

PUTTING THINGS INTO PERSPECTIVE

1.1 – CATEGORY #1: THE CONDUCT

"Who is wise and understanding among you? Let them show it by their good life, by deeds done in the humility that comes from wisdom."

James 3:13 NKJV

To complete this section, follow the instructions in the table below.

General Questions How do they act?	**Answers** Where applicable, if the question is not yes, no, or unsure, write the single-word answer in the blank space below. Total your answers in the last blank below.	**Further Explain the "Observable Behavior" (OB)** Based on your answer to the question, use this section to further explain the "Observable Behavior" (attitudes and/or actions) that you notice in the person. Give examples.	**Your Feelings** Circle the face that describes your feelings toward the (OB). Total your circles in the last blank below.
EXAMPLE: Does the person act mature or immature?	X Yes ___ No ___ Unsure Immature	When in public, I often notice how he pouts when he does not get his way.	☹ (circled) 😐 ☺
Are they commonly outgoing or reserved?	_____Yes _____ No _____ Unsure		☹ 😐 ☺
Are they always on edge or even-tempered?	_____Yes _____ No _____ Unsure		☹ 😐 ☺
How do they prefer to solve problems, immediately or by avoidance?	_____Yes _____ No _____ Unsure		☹ 😐 ☺
Do they behave ethically & morally?	_____Yes _____ No _____ Unsure		☹ 😐 ☺
Will they lie, steal, or cheat to get ahead?	_____Yes _____ No _____ Unsure		☹ 😐 ☺
Do they respect or ignore authority?	_____Yes _____ No _____ Unsure		☹ 😐 ☺
Are they respected or disliked by others?	_____Yes _____ No _____ Unsure		☹ 😐 ☺
TOTAL YOUR ANSWERS →	_____Yes _____ No _____ Unsure	**TOTAL YOUR FACES** →	☹ 😐 ☺ _____ _____ _____

Questions to Consider – WHAT DID I LEARN?

1. What did you discover from the Answers and Observable Behavior (OB) columns? Be sure to note any question that has a negative answer/explanation.

    - General Questions Column:

    - Feelings Column: 
        - What was your total? ______ ______ ______
        - **NOTE: The number of overall faces in a column tells a story. Be diligent to find the answers to your concerns or commendations of this person through additional conversations. Also, use the reference section (Helpful Tools) at the end of this manual for additional support.**

2. List three major discoveries that you learned from this entire section.
    -
    -
    -

3. Add additional comments or questions to consider from this section.

2.1 – CATEGORY #2: THE CHARACTER

"But the fruit of the Spirit is love, joy, peace, longsuffering, kindness, goodness, faithfulness, gentleness, self-control. Against such there is no law. And those *who are* Christ's have crucified the flesh with its passions and desires. If we live in the Spirit, let us also walk in the Spirit. Let us not become conceited, provoking one another, envying one another."

GALATIANS 5:22–26 NKJV

To complete this section, follow the instructions in the table below.

General Questions Are their godly traits evident?	**Answers** Where applicable, if the question is not yes, no, or unsure, write the single-word answer in the blank space below. Total your answers in the last blank below.	**Further Explain the "Observable Behavior" (OB)** Based on your answer to the question, use this section to further explain the "Observable Behavior" (attitudes and/or actions) that you notice in the person. Give examples.	**Your Feelings** Circle the face that describes your feelings toward the (OB). Total your circles in the last blank below.
EXAMPLE: Is this person filled with joy?	X Yes ___ No ___ Unsure	When I am around her, I can see the joy of the Lord in her life.	☹ 😐 (☺)
Is the Fruit of the Spirit consistently displayed in their life?	_____Yes _____ No _____ Unsure		☹ 😐 ☺
Are they Christ-like or worldly?	_____Yes _____ No _____ Unsure		☹ 😐 ☺
Are they modest, honest, sneaky, or greedy?	_____Yes _____ No _____ Unsure		☹ 😐 ☺
Are they peacemakers or instigators?	_____Yes _____ No _____ Unsure		☹ 😐 ☺
Do they seem more like the wimpy or warrior type?	_____Yes _____ No _____ Unsure		☹ 😐 ☺
Does their love and interactions with others seem real or phony?	_____Yes _____ No _____ Unsure		☹ 😐 ☺
Does their public behavior match their private behavior?	_____Yes _____ No _____ Unsure		☹ 😐 ☺
TOTAL YOUR ANSWERS ➡	_____Yes _____ No _____ Unsure	**TOTAL YOUR FACES** ➡	☹ 😐 ☺ ____ ____ ____

Questions to Consider – WHAT DID I LEARN?

1. What did you discover from the Answers and Observable Behavior (OB) columns? Be sure to note any question that has a negative answer/explanation.

   - General Questions Column:

   - Feelings Column: 
     - » What was your total? ____ ____ ____
     - » **NOTE: The number of overall faces in a column tells a story. Be diligent to find the answers to your concerns or commendations of this person through additional conversations. Also, use the reference section (Helpful Tools) at the end of this manual for additional support.**

2. List three major discoveries that you learned from this entire section.
   -
   -
   -

3. Add additional comments or questions to consider from this section.

3.1 – CATEGORY #3: THE CONVERSATION

"Let no corrupt word proceed out of your mouth, but what is good for necessary edification, that it may impart grace to the hearers."

EPHESIANS 4:29 NKJV

To complete this section, follow the instructions in the table below.

General Questions How do they communicate?	**Answers** Where applicable, if the question is not yes, no, or unsure, write the single-word answer in the blank space below. Total your answers in the last blank below.	**Further Explain the "Observable Behavior" (OB)** Based on your answer to the question, use this section to further explain the "Observable Behavior" (attitudes and/or actions) that you notice in the person. Give examples.	**Your Feelings** Circle the face that describes your feelings toward the (OB). Total your circles in the last blank below.
EXAMPLE: Are others excited about their conversation?	X Yes __ No __ Unsure	I have not been around this person enough to know how others perceive them.	☹ 😐 ☺
Is their speech clean and inviting?	_____Yes _____ No _____ Unsure		☹ 😐 ☺
Is the sex topic number one or the Scriptures?	_____Yes _____ No _____ Unsure		☹ 😐 ☺
Is their speech gentle, encouraging, argumentative, or abusive?	_____Yes _____ No _____ Unsure		☹ 😐 ☺
How do they talk to their parents, family, friends, etc.?	_____Yes _____ No _____ Unsure		☹ 😐 ☺
Is their speech free of flirtatious overtones, threats, degrading remarks, and swearing?	_____Yes _____ No _____ Unsure		☹ 😐 ☺
When tough issues arise, will they talk about it, ignore it, become defensive or evasive, etc.?	_____Yes _____ No _____ Unsure		☹ 😐 ☺
Do they listen patiently, or interrupt you when you communicate?	_____Yes _____ No _____ Unsure		☹ 😐 ☺
TOTAL YOUR ANSWERS ➡	_____Yes _____ No _____ Unsure	**TOTAL YOUR FACES** ➡	☹ 😐 ☺ _____ _____ _____

Questions to Consider – WHAT DID I LEARN?

1. What did you discover from the Answers and Observable Behavior (OB) columns? Be sure to note any question that has a negative answer/explanation.

   - General Questions Column:

   - Feelings Column: ☹ 😐 ☺
     - » What was your total? ____ ____ ____
     - » **NOTE: The number of overall faces in a column tells a story. Be diligent to find the answers to your concerns or commendations of this person through additional conversations. Also, use the reference section (Helpful Tools) at the end of this manual for additional support.**

2. List three major discoveries that you learned from this entire section.
   -
   -
   -

3. Add additional comments or questions to consider from this section.

4.1 – CATEGORY #4: THE COMMUNITY

"He who walks with wise *men* will be wise, but the companion of fools will be destroyed."

PROVERBS 13:20 NKJV

To complete this section, follow the instructions in the table below.

General Questions How do others see them & engage w/them?	**Answers** Where applicable, if the question is not yes, no, or unsure, write the single-word answer in the blank space below. Total your answers in the last blank below.	**Further Explain the "Observable Behavior" (OB)** Based on your answer to the question, use this section to further explain the "Observable Behavior" (attitudes and/or actions) that you notice in the person. Give examples.	**Your Feelings** Circle the face that describes your feelings toward the (OB). Total your circles in the last blank below.
EXAMPLE: Is the person motivating?	__Yes **X** No __ Unsure	In his mind he thinks so, but I have heard people say that his speech is often condescending and controlling.	☹ (circled) 😐 ☺
Do others see them as a good, bad, lying, loving, etc., person?	____Yes ____ No ____ Unsure		☹ 😐 ☺
How do their family members view them?	____Yes ____ No ____ Unsure		☹ 😐 ☺
How well do they work with others (jobs, community/ sphere of influence)?	____Yes ____ No ____ Unsure		☹ 😐 ☺
Are they seen as a team player or individual player?	____Yes ____ No ____ Unsure		☹ 😐 ☺
Do they have a network of positive or negative friends?	____Yes ____ No ____ Unsure		☹ 😐 ☺
Do they have a positive or negative influence on their community?	____Yes ____ No ____ Unsure		☹ 😐 ☺
Do you see them as easily approachable?	____Yes ____ No ____ Unsure		☹ 😐 ☺
TOTAL YOUR ANSWERS ➡	____Yes ____ No ____ Unsure	**TOTAL YOUR FACES** ➡	☹ 😐 ☺ ___ ___ ___

Questions to Consider – WHAT DID I LEARN?

1. What did you discover from the Answers and Observable Behavior (OB) columns? Be sure to note any question that has a negative answer/explanation.

    - General Questions Column:

    - Feelings Column: ☹ 😐 ☺
        - What was your total? ____ ____ ____
        - **NOTE: The number of overall faces in a column tells a story. Be diligent to find the answers to your concerns or commendations of this person through additional conversations. Also, use the reference section (Helpful Tools) at the end of this manual for additional support.**

2. List three major discoveries that you learned from this entire section.
    -
    -
    -

3. Add additional comments or questions to consider from this section.

5.1 – CATEGORY #5: THE COMMITTMENT

"Greater love has no one than this, than to lay down one's life for his friends."

John 15:13 NKJV

To complete this section, follow the instructions in the table below.

General Questions Who/what are they dedicated to?	**Answers** Where applicable, if the question is not yes, no, or unsure, write the single-word answer in the blank space below. Total your answers in the last blank below.	**Further Explain the "Observable Behavior" (OB)** Based on your answer to the question, use this section to further explain the "Observable Behavior" (attitudes and/or actions) that you notice in the person. Give examples.	**Your Feelings** Circle the face that describes your feelings toward the (OB). Total your circles in the last blank below.
EXAMPLE: Will she be committed to me?	X Yes ___ No ___ Unsure	Her current behavior of missing special days with me, and prioritizing her job over me, leads me to believe that our relationship will not be prioritized.	☹ 😐 ☺
Is their seriousness about God and loyalty to Him evident?	_____Yes _____ No _____ Unsure		☹ 😐 ☺
Are they committed to holiness, studying/learning Scripture and to prayer?	_____Yes _____ No _____ Unsure		☹ 😐 ☺
Is their job more important than God, their family, or you?	_____Yes _____ No _____ Unsure		☹ 😐 ☺
What are their goals and aspirations?	_____Yes _____ No _____ Unsure		☹ 😐 ☺
Are they driven to achieve their dreams at the expense of your family?	_____Yes _____ No _____ Unsure		☹ 😐 ☺
Are they loyal to and respect their parents?	_____Yes _____ No _____ Unsure		☹ 😐 ☺
Do they love and support their children? (*If there are kids from a previous relationship*)	_____Yes _____ No _____ Unsure		☹ 😐 ☺
TOTAL YOUR ANSWERS ➡	_____Yes _____ No _____ Unsure	**TOTAL YOUR FACES** ➡	☹ 😐 ☺ _____ _____ _____

Questions to Consider – WHAT DID I LEARN?

1. What did you discover from the Answers and Observable Behavior (OB) columns? Be sure to note any question that has a negative answer/explanation.

    - General Questions Column:

    - Feelings Column:
        - What was your total? ______ ______ ______
        - **NOTE: The number of overall faces in a column tells a story. Be diligent to find the answers to your concerns or commendations of this person through additional conversations. Also, use the reference section (Helpful Tools) at the end of this manual for additional support.**

2. List three major discoveries that you learned from this entire section.
    -
    -
    -

3. Add additional comments or questions to consider from this section.

6.1 – CATEGORY #6 THE CONTENTMENT

"Trust in the LORD, and do good. Dwell in the land, and feed on His faithfulness. Delight yourself also in the LORD, and He shall give you the desires of your heart."

PSALM 37:3–4 NKJV

To complete this section, follow the instructions in the table below.

General Questions What gives them satisfaction?	**Answers** Where applicable, if the question is not yes, no, or unsure, write the single-word answer in the blank space below. Total your answers in the last blank below.	**Further Explain the "Observable Behavior" (OB)** Based on your answer to the question, use this section to further explain the "Observable Behavior" (attitudes and/or actions) that you notice in the person. Give examples.	**Your Feelings** Circle the face that describes your feelings toward the (OB). Total your circles in the last blank below.
EXAMPLE: Does his actions show emotional stability?	X Yes __ No __ Unsure	I have noticed that when times get tough, he is always levelheaded.	☹ 😐 ☺ (circled)
Do they know and pursue the secret of contentment?	_____Yes _____ No _____ Unsure		☹ 😐 ☺
Are they satisfied with God's provisions for their life or do they want more?	_____Yes _____ No _____ Unsure		☹ 😐 ☺
Are they consumed with you and your love?	_____Yes _____ No _____ Unsure		☹ 😐 ☺
Are they secure about themselves or are they needy?	_____Yes _____ No _____ Unsure		☹ 😐 ☺
Are they happy with themselves and with their responsibilities/ roles (i.e. on their jobs, in their homes/ community)?	_____Yes _____ No _____ Unsure		☹ 😐 ☺
Are they fulfilled in their career or are they consistently frustrated?	_____Yes _____ No _____ Unsure		☹ 😐 ☺
Are they secure in their sexual orientation?	_____Yes _____ No _____ Unsure		☹ 😐 ☺
TOTAL YOUR ANSWERS ➡	_____Yes _____ No _____ Unsure	**TOTAL YOUR FACES** ➡	☹ 😐 ☺ _____ _____ _____

Questions to Consider – WHAT DID I LEARN?

1. What did you discover from the Answers and Observable Behavior (OB) columns? Be sure to note any question that has a negative answer/explanation.

    - General Questions Column:

    - Feelings Column: 
        - What was your total? ______ ______ ______
        - **NOTE: The number of overall faces in a column tells a story. Be diligent to find the answers to your concerns or commendations of this person through additional conversations. Also, use the reference section (Helpful Tools) at the end of this manual for additional support.**

2. List three major discoveries that you learned from this entire section.
    -
    -
    -

3. Add additional comments or questions to consider from this section.

7.1 – CATEGORY #7 THE CONVERSION

"Therefore, if anyone *is* in Christ, *he is* a new creation; old things have passed away; behold, all things have become new."

2 Corinthians 5:17 NKJV

To complete this section, follow the instructions in the table below.

General Questions Have they been changed?	**Answers** Where applicable, if the question is not yes, no, or unsure, write the single-word answer in the blank space below. Total your answers in the last blank below.	**Further Explain the "Observable Behavior" (OB)** Based on your answer to the question, use this section to further explain the "Observable Behavior" (attitudes and/or actions) that you notice in the person. Give examples.	**Your Feelings** Circle the face that describes your feelings toward the (OB). Total your circles in the last blank below.
EXAMPLE: Is being a Christian exciting to her?	X Yes __ No __ Unsure	I am still getting to know her stance on spiritual matters.	☹ (😐) ☺
Does he/she know what the gospel is & how to explain it?	_____Yes _____ No _____ Unsure		☹ 😐 ☺
Is he/she saved and growing, saved and carnal, or not saved?	_____Yes _____ No _____ Unsure		☹ 😐 ☺
Does he/she actively share their faith?	_____Yes _____ No _____ Unsure		☹ 😐 ☺
Is their changed life obvious to others?	_____Yes _____ No _____ Unsure		☹ 😐 ☺
Is living consistently as a Christian important to them or do they compromise?	_____Yes _____ No _____ Unsure		☹ 😐 ☺
Has his/her attachments to their vices ceased (i.e., smoking, drinking, drugs etc.)?	_____Yes _____ No _____ Unsure		☹ 😐 ☺
When they mess up, are they repentant or non-caring?	_____Yes _____ No _____ Unsure		☹ 😐 ☺
TOTAL YOUR ANSWERS ➡	_____Yes _____ No _____ Unsure	**TOTAL YOUR FACES** ➡	☹ 😐 ☺ ____ ____ ____

Questions to Consider – WHAT DID I LEARN?

1. What did you discover from the Answers and Observable Behavior (OB) columns? Be sure to note any question that has a negative answer/explanation.

    - General Questions Column:

    - Feelings Column: 
        - What was your total? ______ ______ ______
        - **NOTE: The number of overall faces in a column tells a story. Be diligent to find the answers to your concerns or commendations of this person through additional conversations. Also, use the reference section (Helpful Tools) at the end of this manual for additional support.**

2. List three major discoveries that you learned from this entire section.
    -
    -
    -

3. Add additional comments or questions to consider from this section.

PRAYER TIME

Considering what you have learned in all seven areas, take some time to write out a short prayer that expresses your desire for the person you are dating, desiring to date, or marry. Remember to be specific and honest with the Lord and with yourself.

Notes for This Section

Checkpoint #4

Male & Female Specific Questions

Point to Ponder

In Genesis 1:26-28, the Bible tells us that God created the first couple, Adam & Eve, in His own image as "male" and "female." The "image" spoken of in Genesis is not a "physical" likeness, but instead God created Adam and Eve as beings who reflected His mental, moral, and social attributes. Simply put, Adam and Eve, and every human being since then, all possess God's mental, moral, and social attributes. We all have a will *(volition: the power to make decisions)*, the ability to know right from wrong, and a longing to live in community.

While God created the first couple with reflective attributes, He also created them in form and in function "distinctively" different. In their "essence," man and woman were created equally, but in "function" God created them differently (Gen. 2:18–25; 3:16; Eph. 5:21–33). This is a very important factor to know and understand when talking about "male" and "female" roles and expectations in a marriage.

Today, from a "cultural perspective," many lines have been blurred and even erased as it relates to how couples should view and exercise the parental, vocational, marital, and social aspects of their relationship. However, from a "biblical perspective," God is clear on the roles and expectations of men and women in each area. And because His standards have not changed, it would behoove you to talk through these areas before you say, "I Do!"

PUTTING IN THE WORK

Instructions: The list of questions below is not exhaustive but is designed to be a starting point for additional questions and deeper conversations that you and the person you are dating, or desiring to date or marry, should have. The questions in this section are designed to outline the role and responsibilities of the male in the relationship. In this section, the questions are designed for the female to ask the male the specific questions below. Please talk through solutions where needed, and list additional questions.

Questions	Answers	Scriptures
Explain your understanding of work, leading spiritually, providing for and protecting our family.	Was his answer biblically rooted? __Yes __ No __?	Gen. 2:15; Eccl. 9:9; 1 Sam. 25:1–38; Mal. 2:13–16; 1 Cor. 11:3; Eph. 4:28; 5:25–33; Col. 3:19; 1 Tim. 3:4–5; 5:8; 2 Thess. 3:10; Titus 2:6–8
Explain your understanding of the implications of biblical love and how to love me.	Was his answer biblically rooted? __Yes __ No __?	Prov. 10:12; Matt. 5:43–48; Jn. 3:16; Rom. 5:8; 13:8–10; 1 Cor. 13:4–7; Eph. 5:22–33; Col. 3:19; 1 Jn. 3:16–18; 4:10
Explain how you will nurture and encourage me and our children in order to make us more like Christ.	Was his answer biblically rooted? __Yes __ No __?	Deut. 6:1–9; Josh. 24:15; Prov. 1:8–9; 22:6; Eph. 5:25–29; 6:4; Col. 3:21
Explain how you will calm my fears.	Was his answer biblically rooted? __Yes __ No __?	Gen. 2:15; Eph. 5:25–29; 1 Pet. 3:7; 1 Jn. 4:18
Explain how you believe you should honor and bless me.	Was his answer biblically rooted? __Yes __ No __?	Prov. 31:28–29; 1 Pet. 3:7
Explain your understanding of how we should interact together and make decisions.	Was his answer biblically rooted? __Yes __ No __?	Gen. 1:27–28; Rom. 13:8; 1 Cor. 9:24–27; Eph. 5:21; Col. 3:15–17; Jas. 4:8; 1 Pet. 3:8–12
Explain your view of marriage. Is it a covenant for life or a contract that can be broken?	Was his answer biblically rooted? __Yes __ No __?	Gen. 2:24–25; Mal. 2:13–16; Matt. 5:31–32; 19:1–9; Rom. 7:1–3
Explain how we should handle conflict biblically.	Was his answer biblically rooted? __Yes __ No __?	Prov. 15:1, 4, 18; 21:9; Matt. 7:12; 18:15–17; Amos 3:3; Rom. 13:10; Eph. 4:26–27; 6:1–3; Col. 3:12–15, 20; Heb. 10:25
Explain your understanding of a healthy sexual relationship that occurs within the confines of marriage.	Was his answer biblically rooted? __Yes __ No __?	Gen. 1:27–28; Prov. 5:15–21; Song 4:1–7; 7:1–13; 1 Cor. 7:2–5; Heb. 13:4
Explain your understanding of how our finances should be managed and used in ministry.	Was his answer biblically rooted? __Yes __ No __?	Deut. 8:17–18; 1 Chron. 29:11–12; Prov. 3:9–10; 11:28; 15:16–17, 22; 16:8, 16; 19:17; Hag. 2:8; Mal. 3:10–11; Matt. 6:19–21, 24; Lk. 6:38; Eph. 4:28; 1 Tim. 6:3–10, 17–18
NOTE: In 2 Cor. 6:14–18, Paul commanded believers not to be unequally yoked; this is also applicable today.		

2.1 – FEMALE SPECIFIC QUESTIONS

Instructions: The list of questions below is not exhaustive but is designed to be a starting point for additional questions and deeper conversations that you and the person you are dating, or desiring to date or marry, should have. The questions in this section are designed to outline the role and responsibilities of the female in the relationship. In this section, the questions are designed for the male to ask the female the specific questions below. Please talk through solutions where needed, and list additional questions.

Questions	Answers	Scriptures
Explain your understanding of being my helper and the benefits of bringing the best return to our family.	Was her answer biblically rooted? ___Yes ___ No ___?	Gen. 1:27–28; 2:18–23; Ex. 4:24–26; Prov. 12:4; 18:22; 31:10–12; 1 Pet. 3:1–6
Explain your understanding of what it means to submit to my spiritual leadership.	Was her answer biblically rooted? ___Yes ___ No ___?	Gen. 3:16; Prov. 21:9: 25:24; Eph. 5:22–24, 33; Col. 3:18; 1 Pet. 3:1–2
Explain your understanding of how to nurture and encourage me and our children in order to make our home a place of love and peace.	Was her answer biblically rooted? ___Yes ___ No ___?	Deut. 6:1–9; Ruth 4:11; Prov. 1:8–9; 6:20–26; 14:1; 17:1; 22:6; 31:10–27; Eph. 5:22–24
Explain your understanding of how to calm my fears.	Was her answer biblically rooted? ___Yes ___ No ___?	Prov. 31:11–12, 21, 25, 28; 1 Jn. 4:18
Explain your understanding of how to honor and bless me.	Was her answer biblically rooted? ___Yes ___ No ___?	1 Sam. 25:18–35; Prov. 12:4; 31:28; 1 Pet. 3:6
Explain your understanding of how we should interact together and make decisions..	Was her answer biblically rooted? ___Yes ___ No ___?	Gen. 1:27–28; 1 Cor. 9:24–27; Eph. 5:21; Col. 3:15–17; 1 Pet. 3:8–12
Explain your view of marriage. Is it a covenant for life or a contract that can be broken?	Was her answer biblically rooted? ___Yes ___ No ___?	Gen. 2:24–25; Matt. 5:31–32; 19:1–9; Rom. 7:1–3
Explain how we should handle conflict biblically.	Was her answer biblically rooted? ___Yes ___ No ___?	Prov. 15:1, 4, 18; 21:9; Matt. 7:12; Amos 3:3; Rom. 12:18; 13:10; Eph. 4:26–27; 6:1–3; Col. 3:12–15, 20; Heb. 10:25
Explain your understanding of a healthy sexual relationship that occurs within the confines of marriage.	Was her answer biblically rooted? ___Yes ___ No ___?	Gen. 1:27–28; Prov. 5:15–21; Song 5:10–16; 7:1–13; 1 Cor. 7:2-5; Heb. 13:4
Explain your understanding on how our finances should be managed and used in ministry.	Was her answer biblically rooted? ___Yes ___ No ___?	Deut. 8:17–18; 1 Chron. 29:11–12; Prov. 3:9–10; 11:28; 15:16–17, 22; 16:8, 16; 19:17; 31:20; Hag. 2:8; Mal. 3:10–11; Matt. 6:19–21, 24; Lk. 6:38; Eph. 4:28; 1 Tim. 6:3–10, 17–18
NOTE: In 2 Cor. 6:14–18, Paul commanded believers not to be unequally yoked; this is also applicable today.		

PUTTING THINGS INTO PERSPECTIVE

1. List three major discoveries that you learned from this section. Be sure to note any question that has a negative answer/explanation.

    -
    -
    -

2. Were there any areas/topics that seemed difficult to talk through? If so, what are they, and how will you work through them?

3. Add additional comments or questions to consider from this section.

Take some time to write out a short prayer that expresses your desire for the person you are dating, desiring to date, or marry. Remember to be specific and honest with the Lord and with yourself.

Notes for This Section

Checkpoint #5

Extras... Let's Talk About It

Point to Ponder

"Why put off for tomorrow, what can and should be done today..." is a statement that we have used over the years to emphasize the "urgency of the now" ... the importance of not procrastinating or delaying in doing something that is necessary or important. Because marriage is meant to be a lifelong commitment, it is both very necessary and important that you start now *asking* and *answering* as many questions as possible that you have about your potential mate before you say, "I Do!"

Statistics show that *asking* and *answering* critical questions, will give you more of the insights needed to make a better "faith decision" on whether God or your flesh is leading this decision to marry or date the person of interest.

"A fool has no delight in understanding, but in expressing his own heart."

PROVERBS 18:2 NKJV

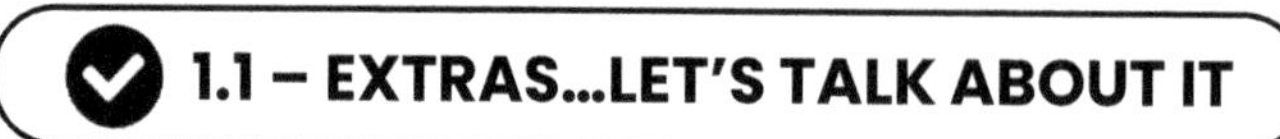

Instructions: Use this section to work through the "Extra" questions listed below, and any additional questions that came to mind after working through the information in this section, or in the previous sections. The questions below will involve both "self-reflection" and "other-reflection." They are not meant to be exhaustive but are instead offered to begin meaningful conversations that can continue throughout the relationship.

Remember to explain your answers and to always provide solutions when possible. Please use the blank space in the margins, or additional paper if needed.

Faith

1. Am I spiritually ready to become involved in a "biblical" dating or marriage relationship? Explain.

2. Do I trust that God will lead me to the right person to date/marry? Explain.

3. How am I displaying my trust in God as I put in the work to discover if the person I am spending time with, is the correct person I should be dating/marrying? Explain.

4. Are they ready spiritually to become involved in a "biblical" dating or marriage relationship? Explain.

5. What are the "non-negotiables" when it comes to your faith and how you live it out daily? Explain.

6. What are your biblical imperatives with regards to respecting yourself as you date/marry? Explain.

Family

1. How much time does he/she currently spend with their family? Explain. Does that bother you/them?)

2. Are they close with their parents/siblings? Explain. Does that bother you/them?

3. How involved are their parents/siblings in their life? Explain. Does that bother you/them?

4. How do you get along with their family now? Explain. Does that bother you/them?

5. Where are the holidays spent in your families? Explain. Does that bother you/them?

6. Are there any other family traditions that your families celebrate? Explain. Does that bother you/them?

7. Will you continue celebrating the family traditions as usual? Explain.

8. Do you/they want to have children? Explain. If yes, then what is the timeframe, and how many?

9. Are there children coming in from another relationship? Explain. Does that bother you/them?

10. What are your beliefs about the frequency and destinations for vacations? Explain. Does that bother you/them?

11. How should household duties be assigned, or does it matter? Explain.

12. How close would you/they want to live to their/your family? Explain. Does that bother you/them?

Friends

1. Who does he/she spend their free time with?

2. How will the two of you handle spending time with and communicating with friends from your past?

3. To what extent will you each require the other to befriend or bond with your own friend circle?

Finances

1. Who should be the primary bread winner for the family? Explain.

2. Should you have "joint" or "separate" bank accounts? Explain.

3. Who should manage the household budget? Explain.

4. How much income is considered "enough" for each of you? Explain.

5. How much freedom should you/they have to spend? Explain. Should there be a limit? Should there be accountability?

Fitness (Physical & Mental)

1. Does your/their family have a history of health issues? If yes, what are they?

2. Are there any physiological issues that will prohibit you/them from engaging in physical activities? If yes, what are they?

3. Are there any health concerns that will prohibit you/them from having children? If yes, what are they?

4. Are there any physiological or health issues that will prohibit you/them from fully engaging in sexual activities? If yes, what are they?

5. What are your views on receiving "biblical' and/or "secular" counseling if needed? Explain.

6. Do you or will you have a specific diet preference that you would like the family to adhere to? Explain.

7. Will they commit to taking an STD examination before marriage?

8. Are you/they expecting them/you to change physically before or after marriage? Explain.

Fire

1. How will we keep the romance in our relationship? Explain.

2. What do you need in order to feel loved? Explain.

3. How would merging your lives together affect dates, activities, and outings? Explain.

4. How will you maintain intimacy in light of interpersonal conflict? Explain.

Future

1. What are the long and short-term goals that you both have for your family? Explain.

2. What are the long and short-term goals that you both have for your career? Explain.

3. What are the long and short-term goals that you both have for your faith? Explain.

4. Do your goals conflict with each other? Explain.

5. Are you planning on living in the city/house/apartment, etc., that you are currently in for life? Explain.

Take some time to write a short prayer that expresses your desire for the Lord to give you wisdom in the major categories of this section. Remember to be specific and honest with the Lord and with yourself. And write a specific prayer for any future conversations that you will have around these categories and others with the person you are dating, desiring to date, or marry.

Notes for This Section

Checkpoint #6

How Do You See Them Now? (Post-Assessment Questions)

Point to Ponder

Whether we would like to admit it or not, we all have biases and preconceived ideas about people before we spend time getting to know the truth about them. And based on our observations, sometimes our intuitions about a person are correct, and at other times they are incorrect. So that is why it is always a good idea to make it a habit to spend time with a person before we begin allowing our own unconfirmed feelings, or the unfair projections of others, to aid in our proclivity to destroy someone's reputation. So, what did you discover?

"The entrance of Your words gives light; it gives understanding to the simple."

PSALM 119:130 NKJV

During Checkpoint #2, "How Do You See Them Now," you listed your initial thoughts about the person you are dating, desiring to date, or marry. Now that you have spent a considerable amount of time with this individual, has your perspective changed about their behavior?

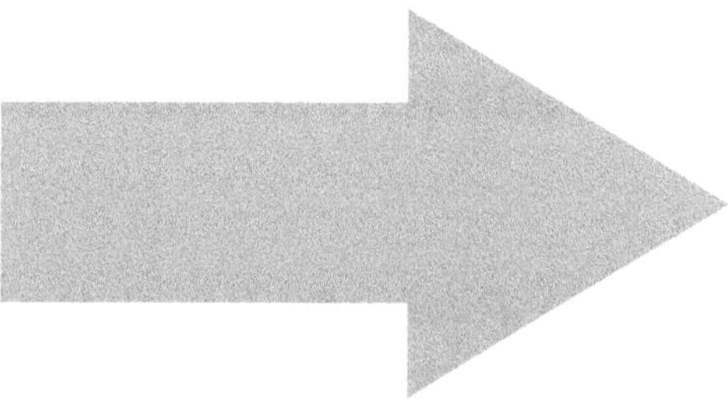

On the Grid Charts, complete Lists 1 & 2 on the next two pages.

Instructions: Place a check by as many areas that describe your current thoughts and feelings about the person since you have worked through the information in the previous sections with them.

Qualitative Qualities	Questionable Qualities
LIST 1	
___ As an attractive person	___ As an unattractive person
___ As a loyal person	___ As an abuser (drugs, alcohol, people)
___ As a family-focused person	___ As an adulterer/fornicator
___ As an active/committed church member	___ As a hit or miss church member
___ As a humble person	___ As a braggart
___ As a charmer	___ As a blunt or direct person
___ As a trustworthy person	___ As a cheater
___ As a conqueror	___ As a complainer
___ As easy-going	___ As a disciplinarian
___ As an informed Christian	___ As a confused Christian
___ As a neat/clean person	___ As a disorderly/dirty person
___ As a mature Christian	___ As a new/immature Christian
___ As a giver	___ As a materialistic person
___ As an encourager/supporter	___ As an envious/jealous person
___ As a good father	___ As a bad father
___ As a good mother	___ As a bad mother
___ As a good family member (sibling, etc.)	___ As a bad family member (sibling, etc.)
___ As a happy person	___ As a miser
___ As a follower	___ As a flirter
___ As a friendly person	___ As an unfriendly person
___ As a forgiver	___ As a resentful/vindictive person
___ As a joyful person	___ As an unhappy person

Qualitative Qualities	Questionable Qualities
LIST 2	
___ As an honest person	___ As a liar
___ As listener	___ As a gossiper
___ As a lover	___ As an enforcer
___ As a leader/influencer	___ As a control freak
___ As good manager of their time	___ As a poor manager of their time
___ As a good manager of their talent	___ As a poor manager of their talent
___ As a good manager of their treasure	___ As a poor manager of their treasure
___ As a missionary	___ As a homebody
___ As an open person	___ As a closed person
___ As a quiet person	___ As a loud person
___ As a responsible person	___ As an irresponsible person
___ As a saver	___ As a spender
___ As one who prioritizes prayer/praise	___ As a nagger
___ As one who is content	___ As a perfectionist
___ As a positive role model	___ As a negative role model
___ As an optimist	___ As a skeptic
___ As an organizer	___ As a lazy person
___ As goal-oriented/over-achiever	___ As an under-achiever
___ As a visionary	___ As a fantasy-driven person
___ As a wise person	___ As an unwise person
___ As a confident person	___ As a worrier
___ As one who empowers	___ As one who enables

PUTTING THINGS INTO PERSPECTIVE

Questions to Consider – WHAT DID I LEARN?

Instructions: Look back at your initial observations of the person in your Pre-Assessment and compare your answers above with those you listed in that survey. Use this section to answer the questions below about your current perception of the person you are dating, desiring to date, or marry. **You may use additional space in the margins or on a separate document if needed.**

1. Since completing the Pre-Survey, what are your overall thoughts and feelings about the person now? List and explain your thoughts and feelings.

2. What were the areas that improved since you took the Pre-Assessment? List them and explain the change.

3. What areas do you feel still need improvement? List them and further explain.

4. What is your agreement on working through the areas that still need to be improved?

ADDITIONAL QUESTIONS

Use this area to list any other questions that you may have that you need to think through.

PRAYER TIME

Take some time to write down and pray through at least three (3) areas that were revealed in this section in which you need more clarity, direction, or peace from the Lord. Remember to be specific and honest with the Lord and with yourself. As you are able, share those areas with someone spiritual who will help keep you accountable.

Notes for This Section

Checkpoint #7

What Have You Discovered?

Point to Ponder

In our busy world that is filled with many distractions, it is easy for us to lose our way, and fail to slow down long enough to reflect on the things that really matter. And because this routine happens for us more times than we would like to admit, we often find ourselves in many situations that we could have avoided, which leaves us asking, "Would things be different, if I had slowed down long enough to acquire and apply wisdom?"

When it comes to your relational future, it is very important to pray and process through as many questions as you have about a potential mate, both individually and with a trusted support system. Doing so will give you time to hear from God, and the opportunity to rest in knowing that you have counted the costs before entering a relationship.

"Blessed is a person who finds wisdom, and one who obtains understanding."

Proverbs 3:13 NASB

Instructions: Congratulations, you have made it to the end of this workbook! You have put in the hard work, and now is the time to summarize all the information that you have discovered from the previous sections about yourself and the person you are dating, desiring to date, or marry. This section is all about you, so take time to reflect on:

- The time that you spent asking and answering questions,
- How you felt as you asked and answered those questions,
- How you feel now about the relationship.

Checkpoint #1: Who Am I?

1. Briefly summarize 3–4 major discoveries that you learned from this section.

    -
    -
    -
    -

Checkpoint #2: How Do You See Them Now (Pre-Assessment Questions)

1. Briefly summarize 3–4 major discoveries that you learned from this section.

    -
    -
    -
    -

Checkpoint #3: General Profile Questions (All 7 Sections)

1. General Questions Sections

    - Briefly summarize 3–4 major discoveries that you learned from all 7 sections in the "Answers" and "Observable Behavior" (OB) sections. Be sure to note any question(s) with a negative answer/explanation.

      »

      »

      »

      »

2. Faces Sections

    - What were the total number of faces from sections 1–7? Add the faces columns in each section and place the total number on the blanks under the faces.

      ______ ______ ______

    - Based on the results of the column with the most faces, what stands out the most to you about the person's behavioral pattern(s)? Is there an attitude to be adjusted or a behavior to be modified, etc.? Explain.

3. Summary Sections

    - List 3–4 major discoveries that you learned from these sections.

      »

      »

      »

      »

Checkpoint #4: Male & Female Specific Questions

1. Briefly summarize 3–4 major discoveries that you learned from these sections.

    -
    -
    -
    -

Checkpoint #5: Extras (Let's Talk About It)

1. Briefly summarize 3–4 major discoveries that you learned from this section.

    -
    -
    -
    -

Checkpoint #6: How Do You See Them Now (Post-Assessment Questions)

1. Briefly summarize 3–4 major discoveries that you learned from this section.

    -
    -
    -
    -

PRAYER TIME

Take some time to write a prayer of thanksgiving to God for extending His wisdom to you as you have journeyed through this workbook. Praise Him for answered prayers, and for how He will continue to direct you throughout your future relationships.

Notes for This Section

Checkpoint #8

Helpful Tools

Point to Ponder

"I should have caught that before I married them… If only someone would have told me, I could have made a better decision!" There are many people who live in the land of "should have," "would have," and "could have" because either by omission or commission, they did not receive the proper information needed to make an informed decision about the person they decided to date or marry.

For those desiring to date or marry someone in the future, or even for those who are already dating someone or married, the Helpful Tools section is a great resource to assist you in your journey.

Instructions: Use the resources below to further your relational and spiritual growth in the areas of dating and marriage. Although the list of resources is not exhaustive, and the links for some of the internet materials may change over time, the information below will give you and others you know, solid information on how to engage in and maintain a Christ-centered relationship.

Books and Workbooks

1. Thomas, Gary. *Sacred Marriage: What If God Designed Marriage to Make Us Holy More Than to Make Us Happy?* Grand Rapids: Zondervan, 2015.
2. Brownback, Lydia. *Finding God in My Loneliness.* Wheaton, IL: Crossway, 2017.
3. Cloud, Henry and John Townsend. *Boundaries in Dating: How Healthy Choices Grow Healthy Relationships*. Grand Rapids: Zondervan, 2000.
4. Arterburn, Stephen, Fred Stoeker, and Mike Yorkey. *Every Single Man's Battle Workbook: Staying on the Path of Sexual Purity*. New York: WaterBrook, 2005.
5. Damon, Chelsea. *Together With Christ: A Dating Couples Devotional: 52 Devotions and Bible Studies to Nurture Your Relationship*. Emeryville, CA: Althea Press, 2018.
6. Santiago, Gabrielle. *Single but in a Relationship with God: Embrace the Single Season without Settling for Less than God's Best.* Tustin, CA: Trilogy Christian Publishing, 2021.
7. White, Connie E. and Philip Wilder. *Single Isn't Second-Best: Shifting the Perspective on Christian Singleness*. Mead, WA: Kydala Publishing, Inc.; Albuquerque, NM: Great Commission Alliance, 2022.
8. Evans, Tony. *Kingdom Single: Living Complete and Fully Free.* Carol Stream, IL: Focus on the Family by Tyndale House Publishers, 2018.

Audio/Video Series

1. Sacred Marriage (Gary Thomas) | https://garythomas.com/resources/video-bible-studies/sacred-marriage-video-bible-study/
2. Kingdom Single (Dr. Tony Evans) | https://store.tonyevans.org/purchase/kingdom-single

Articles

1. Lydia Brownback, "Finding Contentment in Singleness," *Crossway* (article), July 19, 2020, https://www.crossway.org/articles/finding-contentment-in-singleness/.
2. Carol Heffernan, "God's Design for Marriage," *Focus on the Family*, June 27, 2023, https://www.focusonthefamily.com/marriage/gods-design-for-marriage/.
3. Lindsey VanSparrentak, "Godly Dating: 7 Things Healthy Christian Couples Do," *Crosswalk.com*, April 6, 2022, https://www.crosswalk.com/family/singles/7-things-healthy-couples-do-when-they-date.html.

4. Adrian Rogers, "7 Keys To Healthy Relationships," *Love Worth Finding with Adrian Rogers: Profound Truth. Simply Stated.*, accessed January 4, 2024, https://www.lwf.org/keys-to-healthy-relationships.
5. Finds.life, "Here's the Christian Dating Advice You Need," *Life Church*, accessed January 4, 2024, https://finds.life.church/christian-dating-advice/.
6. Sophia Bricker, "What Should Christian Singles Know about Online Dating?" *Christianity.com*, January 6, 2022, https://www.christianity.com/wiki/christian-life/what-should-christian-singles-know-about-online-dating.html.

Contact Us

If you would like to book us or one of our network partners to coach you through your DISC results, or to teach/speak at your next Singles or Leadership training event, please contact us at:

Raise Performance Group
PO BOX 709, Fresno, Texas 77545
info@raiseperformancegroup.com
www.raiseperformancegroup.com

Scan this QR Code to receive free relationship and leadership resources.

www.ingramcontent.com/pod-product-compliance
Ingram Content Group UK Ltd.
Pitfield, Milton Keynes, MK11 3LW, UK
UKHW061702190726
13853UKWH00008B/2355

9 798218 209483